BENNY GOODMAN
CLARINET METHOD

A book by Benny Goodman teaching clarinet tone,
style, technique and musicianship

Compiled and Edited by Charlie Hathaway

INDEX on page 96

A Joint
Publication
of

ARC
MUSIC
GROUP

Music
Publishers,
New York,
New York

and

HAL•LEONARD®
CORPORATION
7777 W. BLUEMOUND RD. P.O. BOX 13819 MILWAUKEE, WI 53213

A-CAP

B-LIGATURE

D   C

REED & MOUTHPIECE

E-BARREL JOINT

F-UPPER JOINT

G-LOWER JOINT

H-BELL

ASSEMBLING THE CLARINET

Moisten the thin part of the reed thoroughly, then place it on the flat surface of the mouthpiece (C), conforming the tip of the reed (D) to the tip of the mouthpiece. The reed is held to the mouthpiece by the ligature (B). Be sure the screws on the ligature are tightened firmly. After assembling the barrel joint (E), upper joint (F), lower joint (G) and bell (H), then insert the mouthpiece into the barrel joint.

TUNING THE CLARINET

Strike the note "A" on the piano or tuning fork. This note conforms with the note "B" in the clarion (middle) register of the clarinet. If the clarinet is found to be lower in pitch than the piano note, push the mouthpiece in further on the cork of the barrel joint. If the clarinet is higher in pitch than the piano, pull the mouthpiece out so that it does not go so far down on the cork of the barrel joint.

For an appreciation of tuning technique it may be noted here that pitch is determined by the length of the tubing in the instrument. Thus, pulling out the mouthpiece lengthens the tubing, lowering the pitch, and, conversely, pushing in the mouthpiece shortens the tubing, raising the pitch.

FINGER POSITION

SITTING POSITION

The Clarinet, invented about the year 1690 by J. C. Denner, and later improved to its present degree of efficiency by Auguste Buffet, Jr., is, without contradiction, the greatest instrument of the wood wind section in richness of tone and extent of compass. It is not only the soul of military music but one of the principal supports of the orchestra.

During the classical period and well into the nineteenth century, orchestral clarinets were made in three keys:

(1) The Clarinet in C, a non-transposing instrument written and sounding in the key of the composition.

(2) The Clarinet in B♭, a transposing instrument, sounding a major second (2 semitones) lower than written, therefore written in the key of two flats less or two sharps more than the key of the composition.

(3) The Clarinet in A, a transposing instrument, sounding a minor third lower, and therefore written in the key of three flats more or three sharps less than the key of the composition.

Of these three Clarinets, the first, the non-transposing C Clarinet is obsolete. This leaves us the choice of two instruments with the same compass of almost four octaves

which on the B♭ Clarinet sounds

and on the A Clarinet sounds

In the upper notes of the high register it loses considerably and the tones are screeching, sometimes very disagreeable to the ear and mostly defective. Those who apply themselves too much to the practice of those tones rarely develop a good tone in the low register (Chalumeau). So, practically speaking it is inadvisable to go beyond the high G

which is the reasonable limitation of the instrument.

The Clarinet is divided into three registers: The first, and deepest, register extends from low

Eʰ to Bᵇ

and the second, and middle, register starts at Bᵇ and goes to Cʰ

and the third, or high, register starts at C♯

and ascends to the high Cʰ

The student, in making a choice between the Bᵇ and A Clarinets may be guided by the fact that there is such a slight difference of quality in the two that not even an expert clarinettist can tell (from its tone quality) whether a passage is being played on the A or Bᵇ instrument. The actual difference between the two is largely a matter of text book theory rather than practical fact. However, the Bᵇ instrument is used almost exclusively in dance orchestras and predominantly in symphonic orchestras.

The music for the Clarinet, like that of the Violin, Flute, etc., is written in the G clef, and the key in which you are to play is indicated by the key signature placed at the beginning of the composition or strain.

The student who expects to enter the field of capable performers must regulate his periods of practice so that the most may be gotten out of them. Very often the student is improperly advised about the routine to be followed during these practice or study periods. Therefore, the following is recommended as a guide for practicing:

The study period should never exceed one hour. Rest at least fifteen minutes between periods and concentrate on something entirely different from music before resuming practice. Good results are impossible without practicing at least one hour daily.

Divide the hour as follows:
  (1) Ten minutes for scale practice.
  (2) Ten minutes for sustained tones, including crescendi and diminuendi.
  (3) Twenty minutes for technical exercises.
  (4) Twenty minutes for phrasing lessons.

In practice, the student should always mark the bars or phrases that seem difficult and repeat them until they are easy to play. Never think of any passage as being "hard" (within reason), but say to yourself that it is unfamiliar and needs more practice.

THE EMBOUCHURE

The manner in which the mouth is formed around the mouthpiece of the instrument is called *Embouchure.* Insert about half of the mouthpiece into the mouth, the reed facing downward. The lower lip is drawn slightly over the teeth, and the upper lip is pressed downward to prevent the contact between upper teeth and mouthpiece. Compress the corners of the mouth tightly so that no air can escape while playing, but be very careful that the mouth is not compressed over the mouthpiece, because the reed must have proper play to vibrate in order to acquire roundness and clearness of tone.

TONGUE ACTION

The tongue is used to start almost all tones and to produce staccato effects. This is done by touching the point of the mouthpiece with the tongue and immediately retracting it. The use of the tongue to start a tone is called *Attack* and may be done lightly or sharply as the effect is required. The tongue should be perfectly relaxed in the mouth when playing sustained tones, thereby eliminating any possible strain.

BREATH CONTROL

Inhaling should be done by pushing out the diaphragm thereby filling the lower part of the lungs. Exhaling should be done by pressing inward with the muscles across the diaphragm. This method, rather than expanding the chest, promotes better breath control and also minimizes fatigue. To inhale while playing, take in the air at the corners of the mouth, being careful to retain the embouchure.

VIBRATO

The vibrato on the clarinet is obtained by the vibration or pulsation of the lower jaw with an up and down motion. This produces clearness and roundness of tone and is a great aid in expression. THE VIBRATO SHOULD BE PRACTICED ON SUSTAINED TONES ONLY. THE STUDENT SHOULD NOT ATTEMPT VIBRATO UNTIL THE EMBOUCHURE HAS BECOME DEFI-NITELY FORMED. Failure to observe this will present difficulties that will be hard to eliminate later.

FIRST TONES TO BE PRACTICED

The following is an exercise designed to develop roundness of tone. The notes must be attacked with a sharp stroke of the tongue and the sounds completely sustained, connecting successive notes without a jerk or a perceptible gap. The notes must have the same degree of power and intensity regardless of the intervals between them.

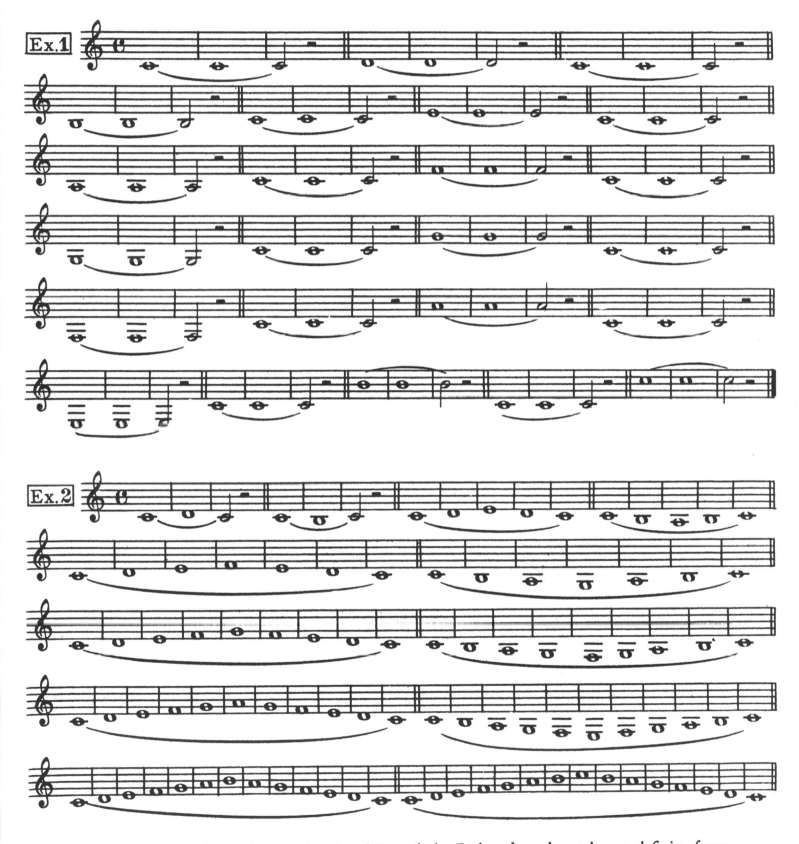

The student should practice exercises 1 and 2 until the Embouchure has taken a definite form.

PREPARATORY STUDIES FOR THE CHROMATIC SCALE

Play slowly and try to give each note a round, full tone.

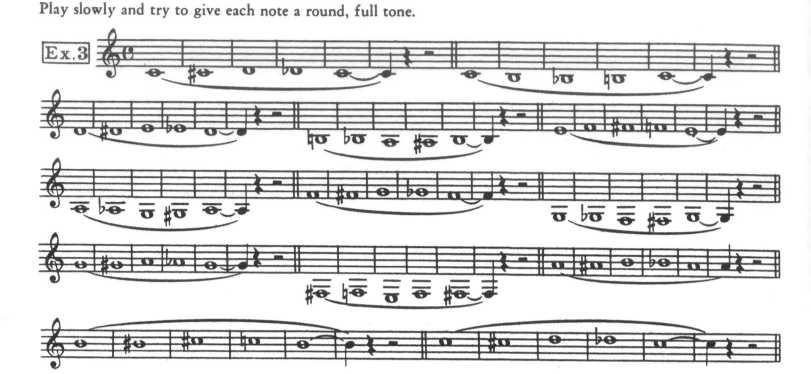

THE CHROMATIC SCALE

Play the following only after the Embouchure is well formed.

SCALES

Most students overlook the importance of scales when, in reality, every good musician practices them daily.

All scales and exercises must be played very slowly until the scale or exercise is thoroughly familiar. Take breath at the sign, (♪).

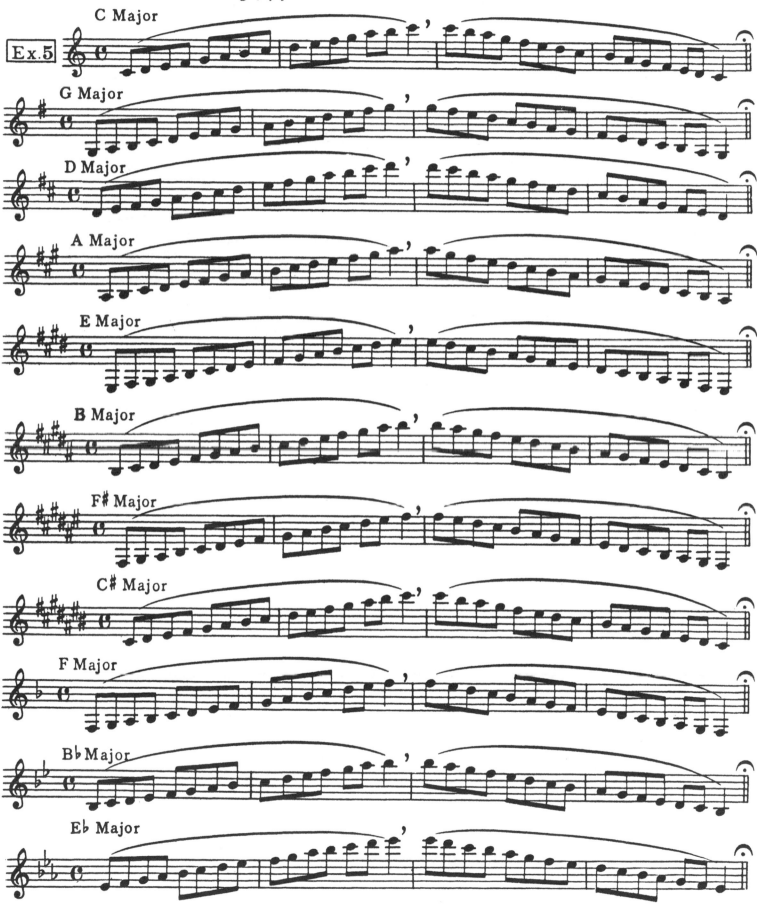

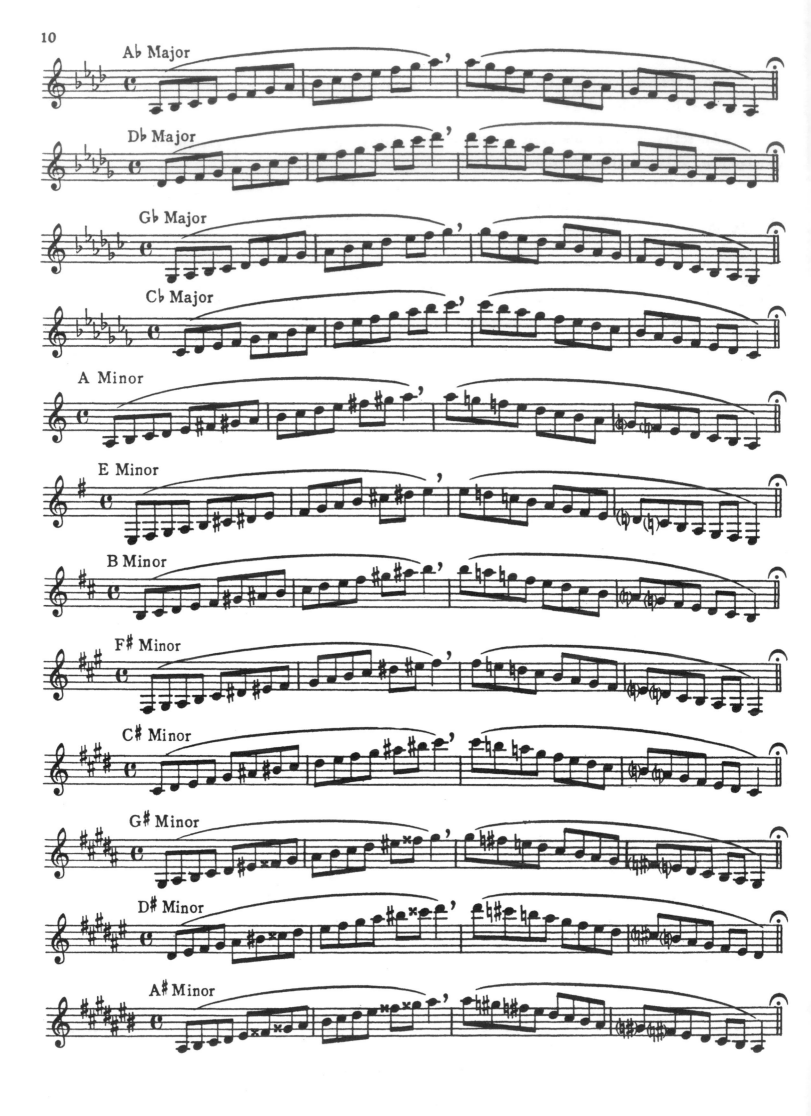

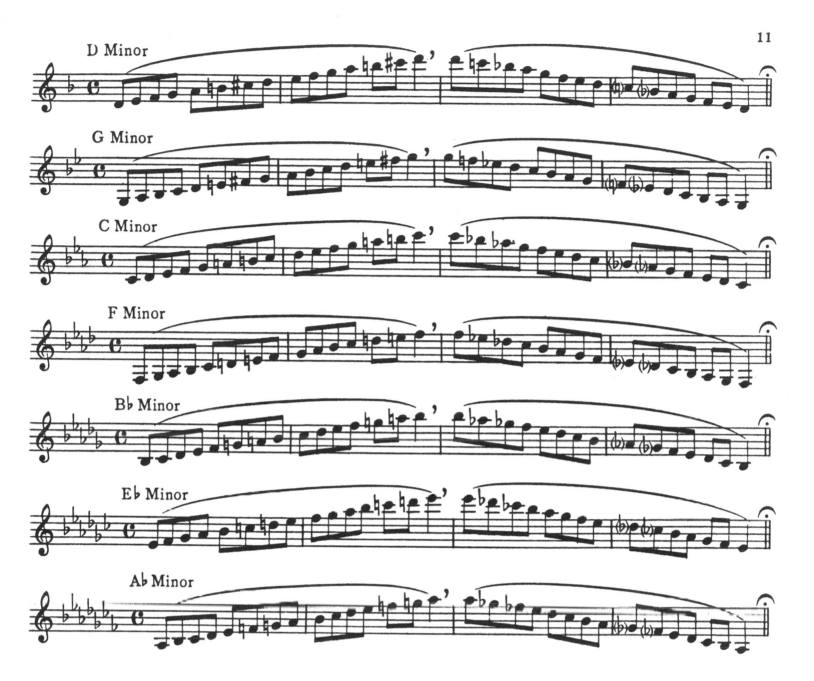

STUDIES IN INTERVALS

After the student has become thoroughly familiar with all the major and minor scales, he is prepared to proceed with the exercises on intervals. This is the principal aid in becoming thoroughly familiar with the instrument and should be practiced until the sounds of all intervals are thoroughly established in the student's ear, as this facilitates recognition of each interval by its sound.

STUDIES IN THIRDS

Thirds must be considered next. Their frequent appearance in all types of music indicates that they are the intervals most commonly used.

C Minor

Ab Major

F Minor

Db Major

Bb Minor

Gb Major

Eb Minor

B Major

G# Minor *(This exercise may be practiced one octave lower)*

E Minor

C Major

A Minor

The following short exercises should be practiced daily. These exercises must be played very slowly at first, and the speed may be gradually increased until all feeling of difficulty has disappeared.

Ex. 8

Play 20 times   Play 20 times   Play 20 times   Play 20 times

simile

STUDIES IN FOURTHS

Fourths are generally considered a very awkward interval and therefore should be practiced constantly.

STUDIES IN FIFTHS

The following studies (fifths, sixths, sevenths, and octaves) are shown not only for technical practice but also to acquaint the student with their various sounds.

Play each of the following exercises until each is free from any difficulties in playing.

STUDIES IN SIXTHS

Play and repeat each of the following exercises as many times as is necessary to eliminate all difficulties in playing.

SEVENTHS (Major and Minor)

Play and repeat the following exercises until perfect ease in playing is accomplished.

STUDIES IN OCTAVES

22

A Minor

D Minor

G Minor (*This exercise may be practiced one octave higher*)

C Minor

F Minor (*This exercise may be practiced one octave higher*)

B♭ Minor

EXPRESSION

Expression in music, sometimes called shading, is of the greatest importance because therein lies the difference between good music and just "sounds" or noise. Expression is to music what the various colors are to painting.

To become adept at expression, or shading, the student must concentrate on the practice of prolonged sounds or "long tones;" such as are found in Ex. 1. This is invaluable aid in the formation of tonal quality.

There is one general rule to be observed unless otherwise indicated. This rule consists of swelling or filling out the sound when the passage ascends, and in diminishing it when the passage descends.

There are five principal expression markings used to indicate the different shades of sounds.

(1) f denotes that the sound must be loud (forte) and remain so until the next expression mark. To obtain this sound the student must attack the note with a very sharp stroke of the tongue and sustain the degree of sound for the entire duration of the phrase or passage.

(2) p indicates that the sound must be soft (piano). To obtain this the student must attack the note with a very gentle stroke of the tongue and sustain the degree of sound for the entire duration of the phrase or passage.

(3) $>$ indicates that the sound must begin loud (forte) and gradually diminish in the degree of sound until it becomes soft (piano). Should the sign appear at medium loud (mezzo forte) then diminish to very soft (pianissimo).

(4) $<$ denotes that the sound is started softly and increased to the degree of loudness indicated. This is, of course, the reverse of the above.

(5) $<>$ is a combination of the two markings explained above. The sound begins softly, increases in volume to the center, which is the loudest point, then diminishes in the same proportion, arriving at the original degree of sound.

The appearance of a line over a note ⌐ indicates that the note is to be held for its full value. The word tenuto (abbr.-ten.) is sometimes used. The appearance of a dot over a note ᴵ indicates that the note is to be played for only a part of its value with the remaining value in rest. Thus the passage ᴵ ᴵ ᴵ ᴵ would sound ♪ ₇ ♪ ₇ ♪ ₇ ♪ ₇

The sign ⊳ known as an accent mark, indicates that the note above which it appears is to receive a stronger dynamic value.

To indicate the different degrees of intensity of sound, we use the signs below:

pp	(pianissimo)	very soft or piano
p	(piano)	soft, subdued in quality
mp	(mezzo piano)	moderately soft
mf	(mezzo forte)	half loud, moderately forte
f	(forte)	loud
ff	(fortissimo)	very loud

Sometimes the sign *ppp* is used to indicate the very softest sound that can be used; *fff* is used to indicate the greatest degree of intensity possible.

A loud sound immediately followed by a soft one is marked *fp* (forte piano), and the sforzando *sfz* indicates that one note is to be attacked in a very loud or strong manner.

The pause ⌢ called fermata, when appearing over a note, indicates that the note is held for an indefinite length; and when appearing over a double bar ⌢‖ indicates a pause of indefinite length before proceeding.

STUDIES IN EXPRESSION

The student should exercise great care in attacking the notes in the following exercises. Let the tongue action be as light as possible when attacking the notes marked *pp*, and more pronounced for the louder nuances. Do not make any crescendos or diminuendos on one note but sustain each with the same degree of sound. When playing *ff* strive for good tone quality. It is the misinformed musician who thinks that *ff* indicates a loud, coarse tone.

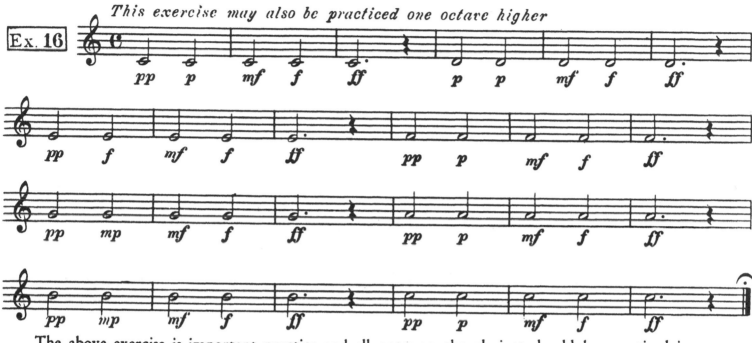

The above exercise is important practice and all notes on the clarinet should be practiced in a similiar manner.

In the following exercise strive for an even tonal quality regardless of the degree of sound.

EXERCISES ON MECHANISM

The purpose of the following exercise is to accustom the fingers, by habitual repetition, to function either separately or as a group. Finger coordination and purity of tone are the features of an excellent instrumentalist and are obtainable by these exercises.

Each group should be played ten or twelve times. To finish the phrase play the note after the dotted double bar.

All the notes should be slurred, ascending passages played crescendo, descending passages diminuendo.

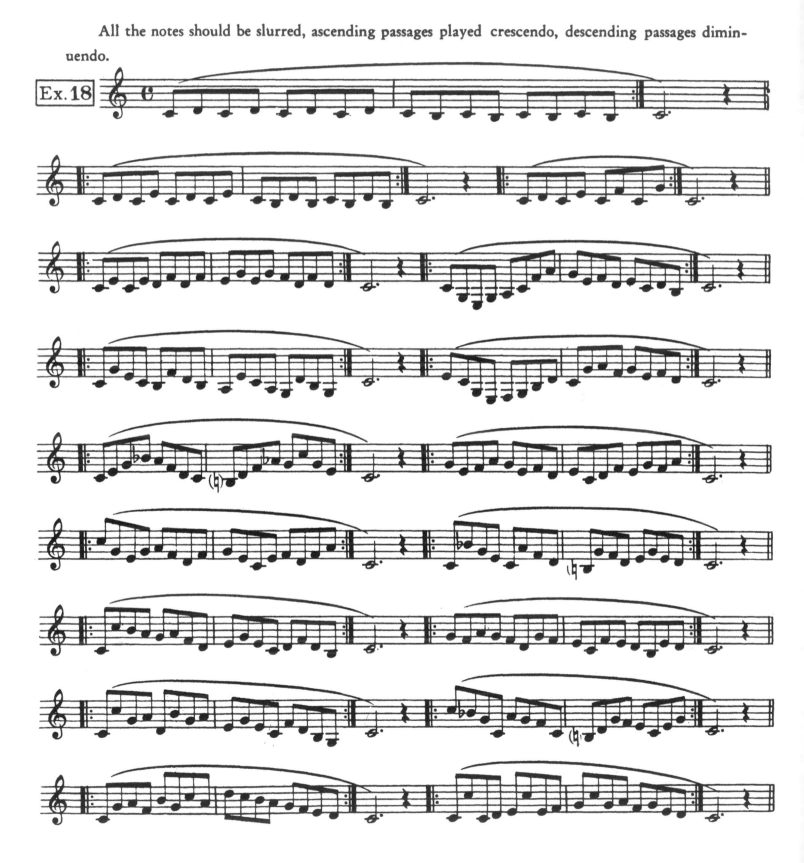

STACCATO STUDIES

Attack each note with a sharp stroke of the tongue. Be careful not to produce a coarse tone.

Keep the reed as free from saliva as possible in order to keep the tone clear.

Subdivide the notes in exercises 22 and 23 into sixteenth notes and play them softly.

The following exercise is designed to coordinate the raising or dropping of two or more fingers on **the** keys or tone holes. First play the exercise without blowing, and watch the fingers; be sure the finger joints are slightly curved, not pointed.

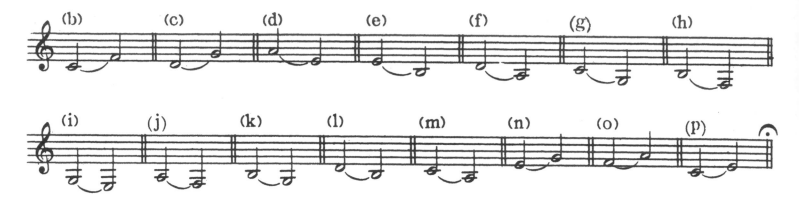

Practice each of the following in the above manner.

Reverse the above exercises by starting with the second note. The above exercise may also be practiced one octave higher.

Play each group several times. Do not force the notes. Too much pressure between the lips and teeth is not good; press corners of lips inwardly.

CHROMATIC STUDIES

Chromatic scales have their own importance, and should be practiced daily. The student should remember to play the exercises slowly at first, and increase the speed as the difficulty diminishes.

(*Play and repeat each of the following ten times daily*)

RHYTHMIC STACCATO STUDIES

Play and repeat each of the following ten times daily.

The following exercise is designed to aid the rhythmic sense of the student. Careful observance of the rest is required. Each note should be attacked with a light stroke of the tongue without losing the full tonal quality.

Practice the following with variations in rhythm such as in Ex. 29

Exercises 32, 33, and 34 are often played with the sixteenth notes sounding like thirty-seconds because the dotted eighth is not held long enough. The following exercise will help the student get the exact feeling of the sixteenth note.

STUDIES ON THE DOTTED EIGHTH AND SIXTEENTH NOTES

The important thing in this exercise is to give full value to the dotted eighth note. The following exercise is a duet. The student would do well to practice this and the duets to come with a fellow student as a first step to ensemble playing.

Ex. 32

Ex. 33

Ex. 34

simile

Rhythm is the regular recurrence of relatively strong and weak beats. In the following measure in $\frac{4}{4}$ time beats one and three are strong, beats two and four are weak. These are known as beat units.

Syncopation is the appearance of notes on beats other than beat units *tied* to beat units. Thus ▥▥▥▥ or more clearly:

It is important that the student use the metronome when available, or, in the absence of the metronome, the student may improve his rhythmic sense by listening closely to different sounds that have a regular recurrence, such as the ticking of a clock, or a motor while running, etc. At first it may seem to take great concentration to beat time correctly and in a steady rhythm, but with practice, it soon becomes subconscious.

In the following exercise the second and fourth beats of the measure are accented.

Ex. 35

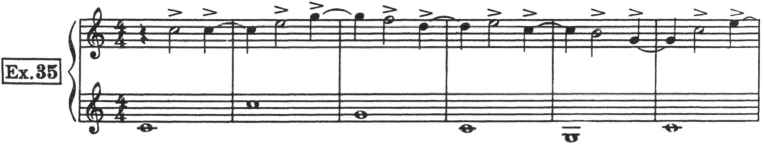

Ex. 36

Exercise 37 shows the accent occurring on the second beat of the measure only, because the ties prevent an accent on the first beat.

The same exercise in 3/4 time.

Taking a breath in the middle of a passage must be done quickly and through the corners of the mouth. In cases like (*) play the note D as an eighth note followed by an eighth rest. The important thing is to come in on time on the next note following the breath.

The following are exercises on syncopation.

For convenience in writing composers usually write the above exercises in the following manner.

These exercises must be played by attacking the syncopation with a sharp stroke of the tongue, detaching each note.

The same exercise in 3/4 time.

The same exercise in 4/4 or C time.

The student should observe the expression marks and always take care to preserve the full tonal quality.

Exercises 43 and 44 can also be practiced thus:

RHYTHMIC STUDIES IN VARIOUS KEY AND TIME SIGNATURES

RHYTHMIC TECHNICAL EXERCISES

The following exercises should be played both slurred and detached. Mark the measures that seem to present difficulties and return to them until ease in playing is acquired.

Study of the Sixteenth Note in $\frac{2}{4}$ Time

Rhythmical Study

Study in Sixteenth Notes

Study in Waltz Time

51

Study in Rhythmical Accents

Rhythmical Study

Technical Study in Waltz Time

Ex. 67

Ex. 68

Study Combining Slur and Staccato

Ex. 69

Rhythmic Study

Ex. 70

Technical Study

Ex. 71

Studies in Triplets

MODERN STUDIES IN RHYTHM

The following group of exercises is designed to equip the student with a foundation that leads to advanced performance and it will be a direct aid to practical playing such as may be found in modern music.

GRAND SLAM

Recorded as "BOY MEETS GIRL" on Parlophone R2757
and on CBS Records, 35482

By: Benny Goodman

Vibraharp

Piano

8va basso

1 At the age of 10, Benny's father takes him for his first clarinet lesson.

2 His first big thrill. He is made first clarinetist in the Harrison High School orchestra, Chicago.

3 He makes a serious study of the instrument under such masters as Franz Schoepp and Boguslowski.

Gone With What Draft

Recorded by BENNY GOODMAN'S SEXTET on Parlophone R.2798
and on CBS Records, CJ 45144

By: Benny Goodman

Gone With What Draft - 2

SLIPPED DISC

Recorded on Parlophone R.3007
and on CBS Records, CK 44292

By: Benny Goodman

4 His first professional job on a Lake Michigan steamboat. The trumpeter of the four-piece band was the immortal Bix Beiderbecke.

5 The big-time beckons. He joins Ben Pollack at the Venice Ball-room, Los Angeles.

6 His first theatre job. In the pit band at the Paramount Theatre, New York.

SHIVERS

Recorded on Parlophone R.2923
and on CBS Records, CJ 45144

By: Lionel Hampton and Charles Christian

BREAKFAST FEUD

Recorded on CBS Records CJ 45144

By: Benny Goodman

7 In 1929 radio hears about the Goodman clarinet. He played with practically every studio band broadcasting at that time.

8 Benny begins to think about leading his own band. To prepare himself he studies arranging and composition under Joseph Schillinger and other noted teachers.

9 His first orchestra playing in the pit for a musical comedy, "Free For All."

10 The first radio show for the Goodman Band. A three hour dance program via NBC Network. Benny provided the "hot" music for the program.

CLARINADE

Recorded by BENNY GOODMAN on Columbia R.3010
and CJ 44158

By: Mel Powell

11 After the radio program went off Benny goes on tour and creates a sensation at the Palomar Ballroom, Los Angeles. Here his music is described for the time as "swing" music.

12 On his way east he stops off at Chicago and introduces the Goodman Trio, with Teddy Wilson (piano) and Gene Krupa (drums). Later Lionel Hampton (vibraharp) was added to make the Goodman Quartet.

13 Always a lover of classical music, Benny joins the Budapest String Quartet for a series of concert appearances and recordings.

I'M HERE

Recorded on CBS Records EE 22025

By: Mel Powell

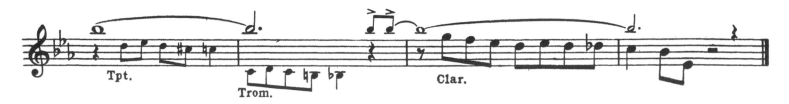

14 Hollywood calling! The Goodman Band appears in "Hollywood Hotel" and "The Big Broadcast", with Jack Benny and Martha Raye.

15 Returning to New York Benny breaks all previous records at the Paramount Theatre.

16 Voted "Best" by polls taken by musical publications and crowned "King of Swing".

SCARECROW

**Recorded on Parlophone R.2835
and on CBS Records, CJ 40834**

By: Benny Goodman

Brass

C Tenor

Brass

17 College students are among the first to appreciate the finer points of modern dance music and the Goodman Band is the favorite of the big colleges and schools.

18 Benny invades Carnegie Hall, the temple of the classical in music, and plays a swing concert.

19 With the Hungarian composer-pianist Bela Bartok and violinist Joseph Szigeti he appears in several concert recitals.

OOMPH FAH FAH

Recorded by BENNY GOODMAN on Parlophone R.3010
and on CBS Records, CK 44292

By: Ellis L. Larkins

20 In June 1940 Benny disbanded this orchestra and took a much needed rest. In November of the same year, he organized an entirely new band which critics and dance fans proclaim is the best that has played under the Goodman banner.

21 The small combination (the band within a band) is a sextet comprising Cootie Williams (trumpet) Charlie Christians (electric guitarist) Georgie Auld (tenor saxophonist) Arthur Bernstein (string bass) Dave Tough (drum) and Johnnie Guarnieri (piano).

22 The crowning event of Benny Goodman's professional career to date was his appearance as soloist with the New York Philharmonic Symphony Orchestra in Carnegie Hall. (December, 1940.)

COCOANUT GROVE

Recorded by BENNY GOODMAN on Columbia R.2767
and on CBS Records 35527

By: Benny Goodman and George Callender

SIX APPEAL

Recorded on Parlophone R.2770
and on CBS Records, 35553

By: Benny Goodman

INDEX